GOD, YOU ARE

20 Promises from the Psalms for Kids

WRITTEN BY

William R. Osborne

ILLUSTRATED BY

Brad Woodard

CROSSWAY

WHEATON, ILLINOIS

God, You Are: 20 Promises from the Psalms for Kids

Copyright © 2023 by William R. Osborne

Illustrations © 2023 by Brave the Woods

Published by Crossway

       1300 Crescent Street

       Wheaton, Illinois 60187

Illustrations and cover design: Brad Woodard

First printing 2023

Printed in China

ISBN: 978-1-4335-8431-2

Library of Congress Cataloging-in-Publication Data

Names: Osborne, William R., author. | Woodard, Brad, illustrator.

Title: God, you are : 20 promises from the Psalms for kids / William Osborne ; illustrated by Brad Woodard.

Description: Wheaton, Illinois : Crossway, 2023. | Audience: Ages 5–10

Identifiers: LCCN 2022023850 | ISBN 9781433584312 (hardcover)

Subjects: LCSH: Bible. Psalms—Prayers and devotions—Juvenile literature.

Classification: LCC BS1430.54 .O83 2023 | DDC 242/.5—dc23/eng/20221209

LC record available at https://lccn.loc.gov/2022023850

Crossway is a publishing ministry of Good News Publishers.

RRDS 32   31   30   29   28   27   26   25   24   23

15   14   13   12   11   10   9   8   7   6   5   4   3   2   1

Contents

To Henry,
that you may know the God
who made you and loves you.

Introduction

Few times are as special for a parent and child as the moments before bedtime. As a father of four, I now look back over hundreds of nighttime prayers, Bible stories, and final hugs and kisses. What sometimes seemed like such a chore at the moment—in the hustle of brushing teeth, rounding up schoolwork, and chasing siblings—already feels like one of the sweetest gifts God has given me and my wife. We have prayed with our kids, been prayed for by our kids, and grown in the knowledge of God together. It is my prayer that *God, You Are* serves to bless you and your children with the same good gift we've been given.

For thousands of years, Christians have reflected on the goodness and greatness of God in the Psalms. *God, You Are* takes twenty "you are" passages from this poetic book and helps children reflect on God's character. Each devotion is designed to explain these various statements in the Psalms, while also helping children see how they point us toward Jesus as the fulfillment of God's word. Each section concludes with a short prayer that is designed for small children to be able to repeat and hear themselves proclaim the glorious truths of our magnificent God.

C. S. Lewis wrote in *Mere Christianity* that all written reflections about God are like a map—they are not the real land. No one goes on a trip and sits in the car looking at a map, while the glorious landscape itself lies just ahead. *God, You Are* is kind of like a map. My hope is that it is a compelling, accurate, and informed map—but it is still just a map. The real thing lies just ahead, out in front of you and your little one. Whether this book is read at night or in the morning over breakfast, or used to help memorize short promises about who God is, I pray it encourages your family to continually marvel at the *real one* and think *God, You Are . . . Amazing!*

God, You Are Holy

Yet you are holy,
enthroned on the praises of Israel. (Ps. 22:3)

I magine you are at a birthday party looking at a table full of snacks—apples, carrot slices, granola bars . . . wait . . . what . . . a *cupcake*. On a table full of okay snacks sits one gloriously delicious-looking cupcake. What do you think is the greatest, or most valuable, thing on that table?

God's greatness is far more than a cupcake's! When we say that God is holy, we are saying that he is the most powerful and perfect being that exists. He is unique; he stands out when compared with everything else. There is no one like God in all of the universe—he *made* the universe! Since he is the greatest and most valuable being that exists, we should honor him, celebrate him, and worship him.

Psalm 22:3 leads us to imagine God sitting on a throne, but not a normal throne for a normal king. It is as if all of the praises of God's people (who are called Israel in the Old Testament) come together and form a praise-throne, and the most powerful, perfect, one-and-only King is sitting upon it. As his people, we will spend forever praising God for his holiness, and we will never reach the end of his greatness.

Holy, holy, holy, is the Lord God Almighty,
who was and is and is to come! (Rev. 4:8)

Let's Pray: Dear God, you are perfect and powerful. You are the one and only holy God. Help me to sing your praises forever. Amen.

God, You Are with Me

I will fear no evil,
for you are with me. (Ps. 23:4)

Being scared is no fun. No one likes to be afraid, no matter what the reason is. But what should you do when you are scared? Hide under the covers? Run as fast as you can? Put your hands over your eyes and scream (like this . . .)?

Psalm 23 tells us what we should do when we are scared. Whenever we feel afraid, we can trust that we are not alone. Doesn't it feel good to be with a friend or a parent when you're afraid? Well, the wonderful news is that the most powerful person in the entire universe is with us! Psalm 23:4 helps us to understand that we do not need to be afraid of anything because the all-powerful God is the always-present God.

All throughout the Bible God encourages his people by telling them that he will be with them. God tells Jacob, Moses, Joshua, Gideon, and David these incredible words. He says, "I will be with you." These strong words helped God's leaders not to be afraid and to follow him. The next time you are scared, remember these ancient and powerful words God has spoken, and know that God is also with *you*.

For he has said, "I will never leave you nor forsake you." (Heb. 13:5)

Let's Pray: Dear God, help me to believe that you are always with me, even when I'm scared. You are powerful and present, and I love you. Amen.

God, You Are My Salvation

For you are the God of my salvation. (Ps. 25:5)

Emergency workers like police officers, firefighters, and ambulance drivers are brave men and women who rescue people in trouble. They rush into difficult places, helping people and saving them from danger. Emergency workers are truly wonderful, but God is the greatest rescuer of all time. He saves us for all eternity!

The Bible teaches us that we were all created to live with God, but like Adam and Eve in the garden of Eden, each of us has sinned against God. Everyone at some point in time wants to do the wrong thing. We want to be in charge and do what we want instead of what God wants. This is what the Bible calls sin, and sin leads to punishment and separation from God.

In Psalm 25:5 the Bible teaches us that God is our salvation. He saves us from our enemies and overcomes our sin. God sent his Son Jesus to take the punishment for our sin so that we can be with him forever. God is the great rescuer!

For the grace of God has appeared, bringing
salvation for all people. (Titus 2:11)

Let's Pray: Dear God, thank you for sending your Son Jesus to save us from our sins. You are the great rescuer. Please rescue my family and friends too. Amen.

God, You Are My Rock

For you are my rock and my fortress. (Ps. 31:3)

Have you ever climbed a big rock? It can be exciting and fun, if the rock is big enough to support you when you climb. Imagine a rock climber standing on top of a rocky mountain. Can that climber make the mountain collapse? No way! No matter what the climber does, that massive rock will not move.

When Psalm 31 was written long ago, people did not climb mountains for fun but ran to them when enemies were coming. They went to the rocks, caves, and heights of the mountains looking for protection and safety. Psalm 31:3 helps us think about God's unshakable power and protection for his people. Like a massive rocky mountain, God supports his people and keeps them safe.

Though the Bible says God is like a rock, we cannot climb on him. But we can come to know God through his word, and we are safe and secure when we build our lives upon his words in the Bible. God is our rock, and his word is our sure foundation.

Everyone then who hears these words of mine and does them will be like a wise man who built his house on the rock. (Matt. 7:24)

Let's Pray: Dear God, you are amazing. You are bigger than all the giant rocks in the world, and you still love me and take care of me. Thank you! Amen.

God, You Are a Hiding Place

You are a hiding place for me;
you preserve me from trouble. (Ps. 32:7)

D o you have a special place you like to sneak away to when you are playing? Maybe you like to go there to play, or just have some time alone. Certain places make us feel comfortable, safe, and protected. When the Bible says God is our hiding place, it is not saying we play hide-and-seek with God! We don't hide from God—we hide *in* God.

Psalm 32:7 teaches us that God is like a special place that we can go to be safe, quiet, and with him. Doesn't that sound like a nice place to be? God, like a hiding place, surrounds us and takes care of us. He is so big that all our troubles and problems cannot get near us when we are hiding in God. Other verses in the Psalms describe God as being behind us and in front of us, laying his hand upon us. It sounds like a perfect place to hide.

When we follow Jesus, we give him our whole life, and we hide in him. Jesus's life becomes our life. We get to live with him forever, because we are hidden in Christ.

For you have died, and your life is hidden with Christ in God. (Col. 3:3)

Let's Pray: Dear God, I want my life to be hidden in you. I believe that you surround me, save me, and will always keep me safe. Amen.

God, You Are My Help

You are my help and my deliverer. (Ps. 40:17)

Learning to do things on your own is exciting. Going to the mailbox to check the mail, fixing your own snack, and picking out your own clothes are all important ways of growing up and learning to take care of yourself. But as we learn to do some things on our own, we must never stop asking for help. No one—not even grown-ups—can do everything on their own. We all need God's help.

Psalm 40:17 teaches us that God is our helper, but what do we need God to help us with? God helps us not to be afraid. God helps us to know what the right thing to do is. God helps us when we don't know how to pray to him. God helps us to be kind to other people and help them. God helps us by saving us from our own sin.

The Bible describes the Holy Spirit as our Helper. When we trust in Jesus as our Savior, God gives us his Spirit to help us live the way he wants us to. The Holy Spirit is God and lives within us forever as our Helper.

[Jesus said,] "And I will ask the Father, and he will give you another Helper, to be with you forever." (John 14:16)

Let's Pray: Dear God, please help me to live the way you want me to live. Help me to obey the Bible. Help me to listen to parents and teachers who love me. Help me to follow Jesus. Amen.

God, You Are My King

You are my King, O God. (Ps. 44:4)

Crowns, thrones, castles, servants . . . these are some of the things we think about when we hear the word *king*. What comes to your mind when you think about kings? Kings rule over the people who live in their kingdoms. So we could say all kings have power, a people, and a place. When the Bible describes God as our King, it teaches us that God is all-powerful, we are his people, and he created us to live with him in his kingdom.

Psalm 44:4 says that God is our King, but we live in a world with other kings and leaders. The Bible teaches us that God is King of kings. He is the King who rules over all the powerful people in the world. He is greater than every military. He is greater than every nation and empire. He is the most powerful ruler in the universe!

God has saved his people and prepared a place for us to live with him forever. The Bible teaches that because God has done so much for us, we are to praise him as our King, tell others about his greatness, and live as people who want to please him.

To the King of the ages, immortal, invisible, the only God, be honor and glory forever and ever. Amen. (1 Tim. 1:17)

Let's Pray: Dear God, you are my King, and I want to live with you in your kingdom forever. You are powerful, glorious, and the only true God. Amen.

God, You Are My Deliverer

You are my help and my deliverer. (Ps. 70:5)

The doorbell rings, you run down the steps, and you open the door. Sitting there in front of you is a brown box you've been waiting for! Isn't getting packages in the mail fun? We get these boxes and envelopes because someone delivers them to us, even in the rain, in the cold, and in the dark. A deliverer carries something to its proper place.

Psalm 70:5 teaches us that God is our deliverer. God is carrying us through the hard things of life to our proper place. As God's people, we have a heavenly address, and God is delivering us safely to our destination. When we say God is our deliverer, we are trusting him to save us from trouble and carry us through coming judgment and punishment.

The Bible helps us understand that God delivered us from sin, death, and darkness by sending his Son Jesus. Jesus is the ultimate deliverer, and he gave his life to make sure that we will be carried safely to God's kingdom.

He has delivered us from the domain of darkness and transferred us to the kingdom of his beloved Son. (Col. 1:13)

Let's Pray: Dear God, please carry me through all the bad things in the world and bring me safely to my home with you forever. Amen.

God, You Are My Fortress

For you are my rock and my fortress. (Ps. 71:3)

What is the highest thing you have ever climbed? What did it feel like to be on something that tall? Have you ever noticed that when you are high up, you can see things very far away? When Psalm 71 was written, people would build fortresses and towers so that they could look out and see if anyone was coming to attack them. The height of these buildings would also provide the people with an advantage over others who might try to take their city.

God does not lift us high into the air like a tower or fortress, but he does know everything that is coming toward us in life and he offers us protection and safety. Sometimes we like to think we are strong. We like to think we can take care of ourselves. When we believe that God is our fortress, we know that we are safe and strong *in him*. Our strength comes from the Lord, our protector.

The Bible explains something hard for us to understand—when we are weak, we are strong. When we can't do things, we remember how much we need God to take care of us and be our strength. When we feel like we can't protect ourselves, we can always trust that God is our fortress!

Be strong in the Lord and in the strength of his might. (Eph. 6:10)

Let's Pray: Dear God, help me to look to you for strength and protection. You are my fortress and my Savior. Amen.

God, You Are My Refuge

You are my strong refuge. (Ps. 71:7)

W hen Psalm 71:7 was written long ago, the mountains were filled with little animals called rock badgers. These cute, furry little critters would scamper around the rocks and cliffs looking for food and shelter. In fact, the Bible describes the rocks as a refuge for the rock badgers (Ps. 104:18). They live, hide, sleep, and find protection in the refuge of the rocks.

While being a rock badger sounds like fun, we cannot live on top of a mountain, and we need more than grass to eat. When Psalm 71:7 says that God is our refuge, it means that we can find shelter, care, rest, and protection in him. When we are tired, we can rest knowing that God gives us rest. When we are scared, God protects us from harm and works good for us all the time. When we feel alone, we can run to our heavenly Father who knows everyone who takes refuge in him (Nah. 1:7)!

God is our refuge, but as his children we do not have to hide away, wondering if things will get better. The Bible teaches us that we have hope in the promises of God. Even when we run to God as our refuge, we can have hope that in Jesus everything will be made right.

We who have fled for refuge might have strong encouragement
to hold fast to the hope set before us. (Heb. 6:18)

Let's Pray: Dear God, help me to hope in you and find refuge in your promises. I love you. Amen.

God, You Are the God Who Works Wonders

You are the God who works wonders. (Ps. 77:14)

God is so powerful that he can do anything. God created the whole world with simply his words. A God who can do that can accomplish amazing things. God's wonders are those things he does that we do not understand. One of God's wonders performed in the Old Testament was making a way for his people through the sea! When God saved his people Israel from the Egyptians, he parted the sea and allowed them to walk through the waters on dry land.

In that scary moment, God performed a wonder-filled miracle. God's wonders are not just neat tricks, like a magician would perform at a birthday party—they are powerful acts of kindness and care for his people.

God's care and love for his people are demonstrated through another amazing wonder in the New Testament. Jesus, the Son of God, comes to us in a human body, dies, and is raised from the dead, showing God's power. There is nothing more amazing than God coming to live among us and overcoming sin and death. It's truly wonderful.

[He] was declared to be the Son of God in power according to the Spirit of holiness by his resurrection from the dead, Jesus Christ our Lord. (Rom. 1:4)

Let's Pray: Dear God, you are powerful and do amazing things. Thank you for raising Jesus from the dead and saving me from my sin.

God, You Are a Shepherd

Give ear, O Shepherd of Israel. (Ps. 80:1)

Sheep are funny animals. They have fluffy wool and skinny little legs, and they eat lots of grass. But one thing you may not know about sheep is that they get lost very easily. If someone isn't looking after them, sheep can quickly wander off and get into trouble—they can fall and get hurt or be attacked by a wild animal. Sheep need a shepherd to take care of them.

Psalm 80:1 calls God the Shepherd of Israel. God's people in the Old Testament were called the people of Israel, and this psalm talks about them like they were sheep. How might God's people be like sheep? Do you think they were furry? No, God's people are like sheep because they need a shepherd to take care of them. We are like sheep too. It's easy for us to go the wrong way, make bad choices, and not live the way God wants us to. We also need a shepherd.

The good news of the Bible is God loves his sheep and wants to take care of them. Jesus tells his disciples, "I am the good shepherd," because he loves his people and will take care of them like a shepherd. Jesus loves his sheep so much that he gave his own life to save them.

The good shepherd lays down his life for the sheep. (John 10:11)

Let's Pray: Dear God, I know I easily forget your ways and can get into trouble. Thank you for being a good shepherd who loves his sheep. Amen.

God, You Are Forgiving

For you, O Lord, are good and forgiving. (Ps. 86:5)

Have you ever had to forgive someone who hurt your feelings or made you upset? It isn't easy, is it? When we make mistakes, we want people to forgive us, but it is not as easy to forgive others when we have been hurt. The good news is that what is hard for us is not hard for God. God is powerful. God is good. And God is forgiving.

When we have done something that we know is wrong, sometimes we want to run away and hide. We don't want people to know what we have done, and we don't want God to know what we have done. Maybe we feel scared of what will happen if we tell someone or talk to God about our sin. Though sin makes us feel bad, we should never be scared to confess our sins to God. He is not a scary God who explodes in anger when we come to him. He is a forgiving God who receives us and saves us.

God does not like sin. It does make him angry. But he dislikes it so much that he destroyed the power of sin and evil. Jesus, the Son of God, took the punishment for our sins and, because we have faith in him, God is no longer angry at us. Through Jesus our sin is forgiven, and God happily welcomes us into his family as sons and daughters!

If we confess our sins, he is faithful and just to forgive us our
sins and to cleanse us from all unrighteousness. (1 John 1:9)

Let's Pray: Dear God, I know that I sin and do not please you all the time. Thank you for forgiving me and sending Jesus to take away my sin.

God, You Are Never-Changing

But you are the same, and your years have no end. (Ps. 102:27)

Do you remember what it was like being little? What were some of the things you couldn't do when you were younger? We all change as we grow. Babies grow into small children. Little kids grow into big kids. But people are not the only things that grow and change. Everything in our universe is moving, growing, and changing—except God!

The fact that God never changes is one of the things that makes him *God*. He is completely different from everything else in the universe in this way. From tiny little molecules to majestic planets in outer space, everything moves and changes—even if we can't see it. God is different from the universe because he created the universe. We might make a person out of modeling clay, but that clay person is never really like us. Similarly, God creates a magnificent universe, but he is not the exact same as his creation.

The fact that God never changes is important because that means that God's promises never change. God's love and grace toward his children never change. And Jesus's power to save is always the same, forever and ever.

Jesus Christ is the same yesterday and today and forever. (Heb. 13:8)

Let's Pray: Dear God, I praise you because you are always the same—good, kind, and just. When everything around me changes, help me to trust in you.

God, You Are Very Great

O LORD my God, you are very great! (Ps. 104:1)

Important people sometimes wear fancy clothes. What kind of clothes do kings wear? What about presidents or military generals? These outfits are designed to reflect the importance of the people wearing them. The Bible teaches that God has an outfit to show us how very great he is! Psalm 104:1–2 describes God's special clothes: "You are clothed with splendor and majesty, covering yourself with light as with a garment."

Can you imagine what a suit made of light would look like? Whoever wore it would look amazing! Only God is great enough to wear these special clothes. Do you think these verses are describing what is hanging in God's closet? Not really. Instead, these images of God's garments are meant to symbolize *how great he is.*

One day, hundreds of years after Psalm 104 was written, Jesus's clothes were transformed into garments of light and splendor. Matthew's Gospel tells us that something happened and his clothes looked like they were made of light! In a special moment with some of his disciples on a mountain, Jesus's greatness was revealed and his followers saw that he truly was the Son of God.

And he was transfigured before them, and his face shone like the sun, and his clothes became white as light. (Matt. 17:2)

Let's Pray: Dear God, your greatness is too amazing for me to see, but I believe that you are glorious and good. Amen.

God, You Are Good

You are good and do good. (Ps. 119:68)

C an you remember a time when you really wanted to do something that wasn't safe, and your parents wouldn't let you? Did it feel like your parents were keeping something fun from you? Did it feel like they were good? The Bible teaches us that God always knows what is good for us and always does what is good. Sometimes in our lives we don't see things the same way God does, and in those moments we might be tempted to think God is keeping good things from us.

We might wonder how evil things and sad things could be good. But think about Jesus. It was sad when the soldiers captured Jesus, when he hadn't done anything wrong. It was sad when they made fun of him and hit him. It was sad when they put him on a cross, and he died. But in the sadness, something amazing was happening. Through Jesus's suffering, God was saving the world! Even when we think about Jesus on the cross, we see God's unchanging goodness.

We might not always understand exactly what God's plans are or how things will turn out, but we can always trust that our God is good and doing good things for us.

And we know that for those who love God all things work together for good, for those who are called according to his purpose. (Rom. 8:28)

Let's Pray: Dear God, I believe that you are good. Help me to trust in your goodness at all times. Amen.

God, You Are My Shield

You are my hiding place and my shield. (Ps. 119:114)

Have you ever been in a pretend sword fight? If so, you know that it doesn't take long to learn that a shield can be really helpful! When Psalm 119 was written, soldiers carried shields to protect them when they were being attacked with spears, swords, or arrows. A shield was important because of how it provided protection.

Psalm 119:114 encourages us to ask the question, How is God like a shield? What do you think? God is not made out of metal or wood, but he is a *strong protector*. God can protect us more than any shield we could ever make. Many times in the Bible, God keeps his people from harm; he is so strong that nothing can overcome him.

When he sent his Son Jesus, God gave us the greatest protection we could ever need. Jesus's death on the cross protects us from sin and evil. Because of Jesus, not only do we know that God is strong and powerful, but we also know that he loves us and is always protecting his children.

But the Lord is faithful. He will establish you and
guard you against the evil one. (2 Thess. 3:3)

Let's Pray: Dear God, you are my shield and my protection. You are the one keeping me safe. Help me to trust you when I'm afraid. Amen.

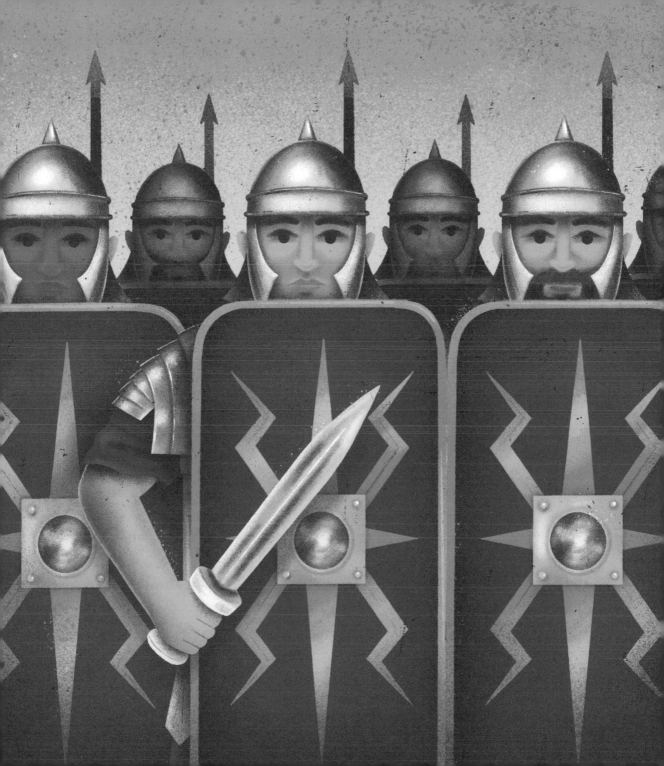

God, You Are Righteous

Righteous are you, O LORD,
and right are your rules. (Ps. 119:137)

Sometimes things happen to us that are unfair. You can probably think of a time when you felt like a situation was not fair. Wouldn't it be great to have a perfect judge who saw everything, knew everyone, and never made the wrong decision? No more, "He got away with it! Why am I in trouble?" We would never have to worry about people sneaking and doing the wrong thing to us. Everything would be right—and no one would have to say, "That's unfair!" ever again. But what about all of the things *we* do wrong? How would a righteous judge deal with us?

The Bible teaches us that God is perfect in all of his judgments and actions. This is what it means to say that God is *righteous*. He never does what is wrong, and his rules are never bad. Since God is righteous, he alone is able to declare people to be righteous. But we often do things that are not right. We call this *unrighteousness*, or sin. The good news of the Bible is that when we place our faith in Jesus Christ, God forgives our sin because of Jesus. Jesus takes the punishment we deserve, and we are given his righteousness. Isn't this amazing news?

For our sake he made him to be sin who knew no sin, so that in
him we might become the righteousness of God. (2 Cor. 5:21)

Let's Pray: Dear God, I believe that you are right in all your ways. Thank you for sending Jesus to take away my sin and make me righteous. Amen.

God, You Are Near

But you are near, O LORD. (Ps. 119:151)

Have you ever felt like God is far away? If so, you are not alone. In Psalm 10:1 the writer says, "Why, O LORD, do you stand far away?" God is so big and powerful that sometimes we might feel like he doesn't really care about us. Compared to nations, planets, oceans, and stars, we are pretty small. But Psalm 119 teaches us that those feelings are not true. God is not too big to be close to his people.

When we believe that God is near to us, it changes the way we live every day. How might you live differently if you thought about God being near to you all the time? Would you make different decisions or speak differently? God loves his children and is near them all the time. Even though we mess up and do the wrong things, God brings us near to himself through his Son Jesus. Because of Jesus's death on the cross for our sins, we can trust that God will never be far away from his people.

But now in Christ Jesus you who once were far off have been brought near by the blood of Christ. (Eph. 2:13)

Let's Pray: Dear God, help me to believe that you are near and that you will never leave me.

God, You Are Everywhere

If I ascend to heaven, you are there!
If I make my bed in Sheol, you are there! (Ps. 139:8)

The Bible teaches us that there is no place we can go that God is not there. Psalm 139 describes this idea by saying that even if we went up to the heights of the heavens or down to the depths of the earth, God would be there. There is nowhere we can go that God cannot find us.

What does it mean that God is everywhere? How can someone be in many places at once? When we say that God is everywhere, what we mean is that he is actively at work everywhere in his creation. Because God's presence is active everywhere in creation, we can be assured that he is perfectly carrying out his will throughout his world.

Knowing that God is everywhere is good news, but sometimes it might not feel like good news if we are not living the way he wants us to. For example, Mommy or Daddy coming home is exciting if we've missed them and want to see them. But we might feel nervous about their return if we know we've done wrong things and will have to talk to them about it. The Bible teaches us that no matter where we go or what we do, our heavenly Father knows and love us.

And no creature is hidden from his sight, but all are naked and exposed to the eyes of him to whom we must give account. (Heb. 4:13)

Let's Pray: Dear God, I cannot hide from you. You are at work everywhere in your world and know everything about me. Thank you for loving me. Amen.

Explore More
Attributes of God

God, You Are My Lord
Psalm 16:2

God, You Are Great
Psalm 86:10

God, You Are My God
Psalm 31:14

God, You Are Slow to Anger
Psalm 86:15

God, You Are My Hope
Psalm 71:5

God, You Are My Father
Psalm 89:26

God, You Are to Be Feared
Psalm 76:7

God, You Are Everlasting
Psalm 90:2

God, You Are Most High
Psalm 83:18

God, You Are Exalted
Psalm 97:9